The Wedding List

By Latricia Bradley

DEDICATION

This book is dedicated to my family,
friends and colleagues.

I would like to thank God
for giving me the vision to write this book.

"I can do all things through Christ
which strengthen me." Phil 4:13

TABLE OF CONTENTS

1) INTRODUCTION

"Would you like to plan your own wedding; however, you are not sure where to begin? Planning a wedding can become stressful and overpowering. This guide has been developed to help you through the course of planning a successful ceremony and reception. It delivers a step-by-step process to keep you organized with a checklist and helpful hints in planning your special occasion from beginning to end." So let's get started!

2) THE WEDDING LIST

1. Vision of the event
2. Create your budget
3. Select a date and time
4. Make your guest list
5. Select a venue
6. Create a seating chart
7. List rental items needed
8. Advertise your event
9. Mail invitations
10. Decide on your menu
11. Hire a baker
12. Décor (style/purchases)
13. Hire a photographer/videographer
14. Decide on event attire
15. Entertainment
16. Transportation
17. Complete a time-line and itinerary for the event

After deciding what you will need for your event, you will need to set a time-line in order to complete your tasks.

We are providing you with an example of a twelve-month time-line and budget. However, adjust accordingly.

3) TIMELINE

12 months
- Announce your engagement
- Determine style and color
- Set a date
- Set a budget
- Compile guest list
- Book venue
- Book officiant
- Recruit family or friends to assist you with coordinating the wedding

9-11 months
- Select Bridal Party
- Send out save-the-date cards
- Book caterer
- Book entertainment
- Book florist
- Book photographer and videographer

6-8 months
- Purchase your gown
- Determine your menu
- Book cake baker

- Book transportation
- Book ceremony musicians
- Buy Bridesmaid dresses
- Register gifts
- Block rooms for out-of-town guests

4-5 months
- Make honeymoon arrangements
- Rent or buy formalwear
- Order invitations
- Order wedding bands
- Hire a calligrapher
- Reserve rental equipment

3 months
- Finalize guest list
- Appoint ushers and other ceremony helpers
- Mail out invitations
- Book your hairstylist and makeup artist
- Decide on and buy accessories for the wedding party
- Finalize post wedding brunch details
- Finalize rehearsal dinner details

1-2 months

- Discuss your vows
- Purchase gifts for parents, attendants, and other special guests
- Have your final gown fitting
- Order welcome baskets (*for out-of-town guests*)
- Have your wedding shower and/or bachelor party (*some have theirs the night before…not always the best idea*)
- Order favors
- Have your bridal shower
- Finalize floral proposal
- Apply for marriage license (*check your state laws*)
- Set-up hair and make-up trial

1-2 weeks

- Call guests who haven't RSVP'd
- Assemble day-of-emergency kit (*maid of honor could do this…include items, such as: sewing kit, scissors, hemming tape, clear nail polish, pain reliever, bobby pins, etc…*)
- Determine day-of assignments for the wedding party
- Call location manager and make sure your vendors have access to the site when they need it

- Finalize seating chart and give it to the site manager
- Check in with all vendors and confirm all details
- Assemble or package favors

3-7 days
- Have your rehearsal dinner
- Finalize all transportation details
- Pack for honeymoon
- Set aside tips for your vendors
- Select family or friends that will coordinate the day for you

Day of Event
- Provide your coordinators with the timeline, itinerary and vendors list
- Eat a small meal in the morning
- Enjoy your day!

After the Ceremony
- Mail thank you cards
- Change your name on your accounts

4) BUDGET

Venue, Food & Beverage 45%

Décor & Flowers 20%

Photography and Videography 14%

Entertainment 5%

Rentals 5%

Stationery 4%

Transportation and Accommodations 4%

Miscellaneous 3%

5)   HELPFUL TIPS – PLACE SETTINGS

FORMAL PLACE SETTING

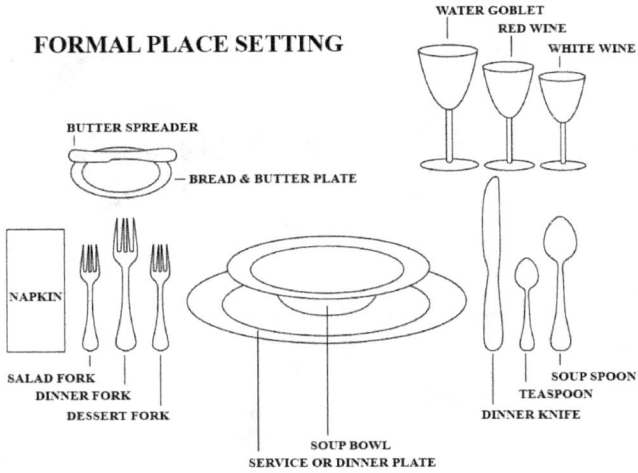

WATER GOBLET
RED WINE
WHITE WINE

BUTTER SPREADER

BREAD & BUTTER PLATE

NAPKIN

SALAD FORK
DINNER FORK
DESSERT FORK

SOUP SPOON
TEASPOON
DINNER KNIFE

SOUP BOWL
SERVICE OR DINNER PLATE

INFORMAL PLACE SETTING

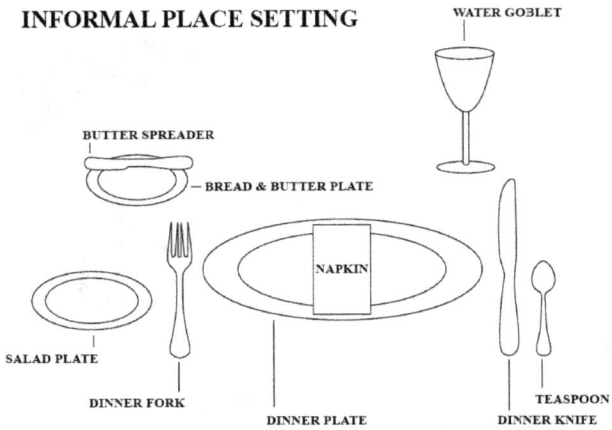

WATER GOBLET

BUTTER SPREADER

BREAD & BUTTER PLATE

NAPKIN

SALAD PLATE

DINNER FORK

DINNER PLATE

TEASPOON
DINNER KNIFE

6) WAYS TO SLASH THE BUDGET

1. Avoid peak seasons
2. Limit your guest list
3. Look for all-inclusive packages
   (*for both your wedding and honeymoon*)
4. Use seasonal local flowers
5. Limit your bridal party
6. Hire a DJ versus a Band
   (*Ask a family member or friend to DJ*)
7. Ask a family member or friend to be the Photographer/Videographer (*give them a curfew*)
8. Hire transportation for a grand entrance or exit versus being on stand-by
9. Limit alcohol to beer, wine and a couple of specialty drinks (*for a seated dinner, consider limiting the number of bottles served per table.*)
10. Do-it-yourself invitations/decorations
11. Print all stationery digitally. Go for great color and typography
12. If using a venue, ask the site manager if there are other events that same day and possibly piggy back off their menu

Do you already have everything you need? In lieu of a traditional gift if you would like assistance with your honeymoon. Direct your guest to sites where you may set-up honeymoon wishes.

7) DINNER STYLES

Buffet – Guests serve themselves
- Cost $
- Pros – Encourages mingling
- Cons – Long lines, things may get sloppy, the more choices higher the costs

Seated – Wait-staff brings plated dinners or family style platters to seated guests
- Cost $$
- Pros – Elegant and formal; everyone eats at the same time, it's easier to control the flow
- Cons – Restricts mingling, may require more wait-staff

Stations- Chef-manned stations
- Cost $$$
- Pros – Personalizes the dining experience
- Cons – Often the most expensive Option

8) SEATING

- **Cocktail** – High-top tables for two or four are great for the perimeter of the dance floor. Guests will tend to mingle.
- **Rectangular** – Gives the feel of being at a restaurant and less like a banquet.
- **Round** – Sense of intimacy, you can see and talk to everyone.
- **Square** – If you decide to have both rectangles and rounds, it can help to break things up.

When using a venue, ask the site manager if they have a blank floor plan. Also, ask if they have any common floor plans. It's possible you may like one of those. You can design a seating chart on the computer.

Seating Option:

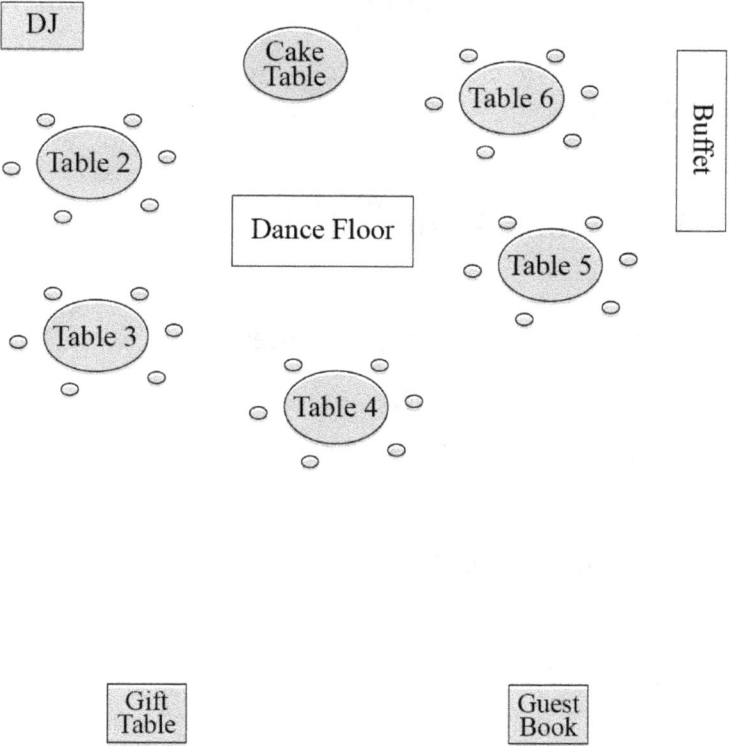

DJ

Cake Table

Table 6

Buffet

Table 2

Dance Floor

Table 5

Table 3

Table 4

Gift Table

Guest Book

Create your customized seating chart by visiting
http://www.weddingmapper.com/guests/demo_seating

9) SELECTION OF VENDORS

(When using vendors, be sure to have a signed contract with detailed information of services to be rendered.)

Cake Baker –

- ❑ Who will bake my cake?

- ❑ What are my filling choices?

- ❑ Do you customize cakes?

- ❑ How far in advance will the cake be prepared?

- ❑ How are your cakes priced?

- ❑ Are you licensed by the state?

Cake Baker: _____

Address: _____

Contact Person: _____

Deposit Due Date: _____

Final Payment Date: _____

Total Cost: _____

Set-up time: _____

Clean-up time: _____

Calligrapher –

❑ Are you a trained calligrapher?

❑ How are your rates calculated?

❑ What is the turn-around time?

❑ Do you have a portfolio that I may view?

Calligrapher: _____

Address: _____

Deposit Due Date: _____

Final Payment Date: _____

Total Cost: _____

Notes for services to be rendered:

_____

_____

_____

_____

_____

Caterer –

- ❏ What is your per person charge?
- ❏ How many menus are there to choose from?
- ❏ How many guests do you overestimate for?
- ❏ Do you allow food to be taken home?
- ❏ Will the gratuity be included in the final cost?
- ❏ How many hours are included in the service?
- ❏ Is there an overtime charge?
- ❏ Do you provide staff to include bartenders?
- ❏ Is the set-up and cleanup included in the price?
- ❏ Do you provide chairs, flatware, linens, napkins and tables?
- ❏ Is there a charge to cut and serve the cake?
- ❏ Who will be the staff person in charge?
- ❏ How far in advance, will you need the final count?
- ❏ What payment arrangements do you require?

Caterer: _____

Address: _____

Contact Person: _____

Deposit Due Date: _____

Final Payment Date: _____

Total Cost: _____

Set-up time: _____

Clean-up time: _____

Menu:

Meats: _____

Vegetables: _____

Starch: _____

Bread: _____

Drinks: _____

Notes: _____

Entertainment –

❏ Will someone from your staff provide service as our Emcee?

❏ What are your set-up time requirements?

❏ How will you be dressed for the event?

❏ How far in advance do you need the playlist?

Entertainment Company: _____

Address: _____

Deposit Due Date: _____

Final Payment Date: _____

Total Cost: _____

Set-up Time: _____

End Time: _____

Notes for services to be rendered:

_____

_____

_____

_____

Florist –

- ❑ When do the flowers need to be ordered?

- ❑ How many people will be available to work my event?

- ❑ Do you have a portfolio that I may view?

- ❑ How will the flowers be stored once arranged?

- ❑ When will the flowers be delivered and set-up?

- ❑ Who will be the staff person in charge?

- ❑ Will you be able to preserve the flowers?

- ❑ Will the flowers be displayed in items that need to be returned?

Flower Company: _____

Address: _____

Deposit Due Date: _____

Final Payment Date: _____

Total Cost: _____

Set-up Time: _____

Total number of Flowers: _____

Types of Flowers:

_____

_____

_____

_____

Photographer/Videographer –

- ❏ Will the person I meet with, be the person that will shoot the event?

- ❏ What kind of lighting do you require?

- ❏ Will you have a backup camera?

- ❏ How many hours will you be available?

- ❏ How are your rates calculated?

- ❏ What is the minimum order requirement?

- ❏ What is the turn-around time on proofs?

- ❏ How will you be dressed for the event?

- ❏ Do you have budget conscience packets?

Photography/Videographer Company: _____

Address: _____

Deposit Due Date: _____

Final Payment Date: _____

Total Cost: _____

Set-up Time: _____

End Time: _____

Picture List:

_____

_____

_____

_____

Transportation –

❑   What kind of vehicles do you have for hire?

❑   How are your fees calculated?

❑   What time will the driver arrive?

❑   Will the driver stay in the vicinity of the event?

Transportation Company: _____

Address: _____

Driver Contact: _____

Deposit Due Date: _____

Final Payment Date: _____

Total Cost: _____

Pick-up Time: _____

Drop-off Time: _____

Notes for services to be rendered:

_____

_____

_____

_____

_____

Venues –

- [ ] What is the rental fee and hours available?
- [ ] What is the sitting and standing capacity?
- [ ] Is there a dressing room available?
- [ ] Does the venue require a membership to rent the facility?
- [ ] What are the requirements and restrictions?
- [ ] How much time is allowed for set-up and cleanup?
- [ ] What is the parking capacity?
- [ ] Are handicapped facilities available?
- [ ] How many outlets are there for Audio/Visual?
- [ ] What are the cleanup requirements?
- [ ] Do you have your own event coordinator?
- [ ] Do you allow outside alcohol?

Venue Site: _____

Address: _____

Phone Number: _____

Site Manager: _____

Date and Time Room Reserved: _____

Deposit Due Date: _____

Final Payment Date: _____

Total Cost: _____

Number of guests: _____

Set-up Instructions:

_____

_____

_____

_____

_____

10) ITINERARY

7.5 hours prior to the ceremony

- Everyone should have something to eat
- Ladies should be getting their hair done
  Ladies: To save time, please complete your bath/showers before your hair and makeup are done.

6 hour

- The bride should have her make-up applied

4.5 hour

- The ceremony preparations begin at the ceremony location. The florist should be dropping off boutonnieres, corsages, and decorations to the ceremony site.

4 hour

- The bride, her maid of honor, her bridesmaids, junior bridesmaid and the flower girl should be at the designated place to get dressed. (*This will allow them to be unrushed*) include the bride's cell phone number here.

3.5 hour

- The groom and his groomsmen will arrive at the designated location to get dressed. List Groom's cell phone number.

3 hour

- Provided separate flowers are ordered for the bride…the florist will deliver personal flowers to the brides' location to include the father of the bride boutonniere. Any leftovers are to be brought to the ceremony.

2 hour

- **The bride should be dressed at this time.** List the photographer name and contact information here. At this time, the bride, her mother, her father and her attendants should be a part of these photographs. Everyone needs to be ready.

1.15 hour

- The bride's photo session ends. The photographer should be getting ready for the ceremony set up. The bride and her attendants should provide someone with any medication, shoes, etc …needed to be at the ceremony or reception.

- The groom and his attendants should be leaving their location to arrive to the ceremony site. All boutonnieres and corsages will be pinned upon arrival at the ceremony site.

1.05 hour
- Everyone in the bridal party should be ready to step into the limousine as soon as it arrives.

1 hour
- The groom's mother and other significant family will arrive at the church for a few pre-wedding photos with the groom.

- Videographer should begin setting up.

- One white, 12-passenger limousine leaves, transporting the bride her mother, her father, and her attendants.

- The hostesses, vocalists, audio technician, readers, ushers, and pastor should arrive at the ceremony site. Please advise your person of contact when you have arrived, just in case he or she needs to share some last minute things with you. The musical prelude will begin shortly thereafter and will continue as the guests are being seated.

.20min

- The bride and her attendants arrive at the church. Please remain in the limo until a person of contact comes for you. We need to avoid getting makeup or soil on you.

.10min

- The groom, his parents, and his attendants are at the ceremony site and secluded from the guests.

.05min

- The processional lineup begins, as follows: Grandparents, groom's mother, bride's mother, attendants, bride and her father.
  (*Note: Once the Groom's Mother gets to the end of the isle they will proceed to light the tapers, then take their seat*)

.00min

- PROCESSION BEGINS AFTER THE OPENING PRAYER

11) WEDDING DAY

1. After the recessional, there will be a receiving line, with just the bride and groom leading to the reception hall. (*Bride and Groom should have informed additional family members they want to stick around for pictures*)

2. After the cocktails (7:00p.m. – 7:30p.m.), the bridal party and parents will be lined up and officially introduced as they enter the dining room before the bride and groom enter.

3. The reception order will be:
   A. Introductions will be done by
      _____ at (*7:30p.m.*).
   B. Customary family traditions
   C. First dance by the bride and groom (*7:40p.m.*).
      a. Title of the song:_____
   D. Blessing of the food by: _____
      (*7:45p.m.*)
   E. Toast to the newlyweds by the Best Man and Maid of Honor (*7:50 p.m.*)
   F. The meal is served (*8:00 p.m.*)

G. Special Dances (*8:15 p.m.*)

    a. Bride and Father (song and artist)

    b. Groom and Sister (song and artist)

H. Tossing of the bouquet and garter (*8:50 p.m.*) (*whomever catches the bouquet and garter must come back to the dance floor*)

I. Cake cutting (9:00) Bride and Groom mingle with guest… (*They may not have talked to everyone in the receiving line.*)

    After the bride and groom cut the first slice, the catering staff will cut, plate and display the cake for the guests to enjoy.

J. Dance floor officially opens 9:30

K. The couple will prepare to leave at 10:25

    a. Reception Music is provided by

    DJ: _____

Notes

Notes

Notes

Notes

Notes

ACKNOWLEDGMENTS

The author wishes to express sincere appreciation to her family, friends and colleagues who encouraged and supported her along the way.

ABOUT THE AUTHOR

Latricia Bradley is a retired member of the United States military serving honorably for 21 years. During this time serving her country, Mrs. Bradley has earned both Accounting and Finance degrees to include a Master's in Business Administration. Mrs. Bradley is a certified event planner and wedding specialist who is now expanding her talent to photography, where she is currently pursuing a fifth degree.